C000282654

The Language of Wild Flowers

A Treasury of Verse and Prose
Scented by Penhaligon's

Beatrice Parsons

The Language of Wild Flowers

Sheila Pickles

A Treasury of Verse and Prose
Scented by Penhaligon's

LONDON MCMXCV

For Joan Weir
My Godmother, Aunt and a great gardener

INTRODUCTION

Dear Reader,

This book should be read for idle pleasure, and is not intended for specialists: it deals with the familiar rather than the rare. You may ask why some of your favourite wild flowers have been excluded. My reply is that many wild flowers, such as Daffodils, Forget-me-nots, Hollyhocks and Lilies-of-the-Valley, are no longer thought of as truly wild and are often found in our gardens. They were also included in my previous book, *The Language of Flowers*.

Wild flowers are generally treated as the Cinderellas of nature; nurserymen and women would argue that they are smaller, have less scent and bloom for a shorter period than garden flowers. However, wild flowers are essential to homeopathy and herbalism, centuries-old combinations of botany and medicine which are practised to this day.

Compiling this book made me realize that I am only skimming the surface. The works of the great Elizabethan herbalist John Gerard and of John Parkinson (botanist to Charles I), contain information about the medicinal properties of the plants, and include their botanical classification as well as traditional plant lore. It is the latter I find most fascinating. The names of many plants are derived from their use in medicine; classical names often embody ancient traditions; and country names often stem from some peculiarity in the look of the plant. The Victorians must have used a combination of all these when they came to select the meanings for the Language of Flowers.

The Language of Flowers was a custom made fashionable in Victorian times. Inspired by a book by Madame de la Tour, *Le Langage des Fleurs*, the Victorians adopted the custom of giving flowers a meaning. The choice of flower was therefore highly significant when sending a bunch to a friend or a lover. The manner of presentation was also significant. For example, if the flowers were handed over upside-down the meaning was reversed. The recipients could respond by wearing the flowers in different ways: on their heart meant love and in their hair implied caution.

I hope that this book will help you to recall something of the child's delight in our wild flora. These familiar wild flowers, each having its character formed by the surrounding hedgerows and furrowed fields, are the mother tongue of our imagination; as an adult our memory is laden with all the small associations our childhood left behind. The sight of sunshine on a field of wild flowers today might briefly relieve an adult's habitual weariness, but combined with a memory of the same sight years ago which still lives in us, can transform that feeling into joy.

It has been a pleasure to collect and select these flowers. I hope that readers will also enjoy some of the poetry gathered to accompany them. There are still many people, I think, who care for literature and wild flowers, and these things belong to the heart of England.

I have scented the endpapers of this treasury with Penhaligon's Bluebell. For me it captures quite perfectly the strong green woody scent of these beautiful woodland flowers. If I can bring back some of the associations from the fleeting hours of your childhood as you turn the leaves, then my work will not have been in vain.

Sheila Pickles, London, 1995

CONTENTS

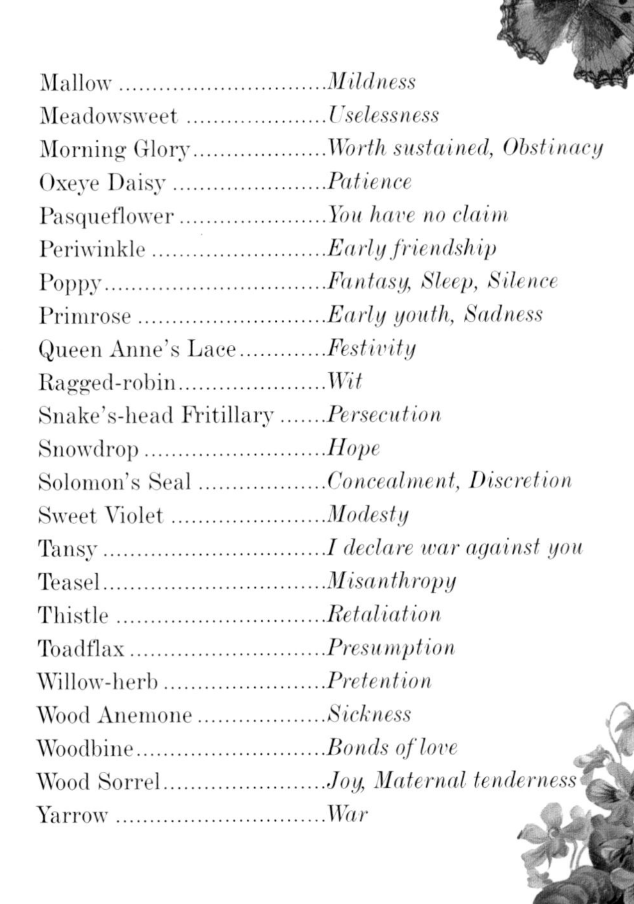

Mallow ....*Mildness*
Meadowsweet ....*Uselessness*
Morning Glory.....................*Worth sustained, Obstinacy*
Oxeye Daisy ....*Patience*
Pasqueflower ....*You have no claim*
Periwinkle ....*Early friendship*
Poppy..................................*Fantasy, Sleep, Silence*
Primrose ....*Early youth, Sadness*
Queen Anne's Lace.............*Festivity*
Ragged-robin.......................*Wit*
Snake's-head Fritillary ....*Persecution*
Snowdrop ....*Hope*
Solomon's Seal ....*Concealment, Discretion*
Sweet Violet ....*Modesty*
Tansy ....*I declare war against you*
Teasel..................................*Misanthropy*
Thistle ....*Retaliation*
Toadflax ....*Presumption*
Willow-herb ....*Pretention*
Wood Anemone ....*Sickness*
Woodbine.............................*Bonds of love*
Wood Sorrel.........................*Joy, Maternal tenderness*
Yarrow ....*War*

Aaron's Rod

Verbascum thapsus

COMFORT

And medicinal betony,
By thy woodside railing, reeves
With antique mullein's flannel-leaves.
These, though mean, the flowers of waste,
Planted here in nature's haste,
Display to the discerning eye,
Her loved, wild variety.

'COWPER GREEN' JOHN CLARE (1793–1864)

AARON'S Rod is a stately biennial plant with large, pale, downy leaves. It grows up to five feet tall and stands on sunny banks of sandy soil. *Verbascum* is probably a corruption of the Latin *barbascum*, or bearded plant, as the mulleins have downy foliage and wide, woolly leaves. The leaves were once used by poor country folk to line their shoes to keep their feet warm in wintertime and protect them on rough roads. This is probably where the meaning 'comfort' arose. Another old name was High-taper or Torch-plant, for the thick stems were dipped in tallow or suet and were used to provide light as far back as Roman times, when the plant was known as *Candelaria*. In some parts of Britain the plant is known as Figwort – the leaves were wrapped around figs to keep the fruit soft and moist. Aaron's Rod also used to provide comfort in an old remedy for earache, for which mullein oil was made by steeping the flowers in olive oil and exposing them to sunlight.

AGRIMONY

Agrimonia eupatoria

GRATITUDE

Next these here Egremony is,
That helps the serpent's biting.

'MUSES' ELYSIUM' MICHAEL DRAYTON (1563–1631)

ALSO known as Cockle Burr, this ancient plant with tall yellow spikes has grown since Anglo-Saxon times in hedgerows and open woodland, and has been used to heal wounds and treat snake-bite. The 15th-century poet Chaucer recommended its use for a bad back, and Gerard, the Elizabethan herbalist, described it as 'good for naughty livers'; it is an old springtime tonic for cleansing the system. The flowers and roots smell of ripe apricots and the leaves are used in herbal teas. The name comes from *agremone*, a word given by the Greeks to plants which were healing to the eyes; *Eupatoria* refers to Mithridates Eupator, a king who was a renowned herbalist, who gave his name to the plant species after successfully using it in medicine.

Agrimonia odorata has a potent astringent scent with a hint of turpentine and was used to make a rough country beer. The fragrance remains long after the plant has been dried. Since Elizabethan times Agrimony has been used in scented pillows and pot-pourris.

BEAR'SFOOT

Helleborus foetidus

——— SCANDAL, CALUMNY ———

Borage and hellebore fill two scenes,
Sovereign plants to purge the veins
Of melancholy, and cheer the heart
Of those black fumes which make it smart.

THE ANATOMY OF MELANCHOLY ROBERT BURTON (1577–1640)

BEAR'SFOOT is also known as Stinking Hellebore for its strong unpleasant scent when touched. It grows in damp meadows and woodlands in the early spring, its pretty lime-green flowers hanging down like bells. In ancient times the plant was thought to be a lucky charm and was used in a rite to bless cattle against evil. Melampus, a soothsayer and physician who lived 1400 years before Christ used it as a purgative for insanity. It is closely related to the Christmas Rose, *Helleborus niger*.

BLUEBELL

Endymion non-scriptus

CONSTANCY

And the hyacinth purple, white and blue
Which flung from its bells a sweet peel anew
Of music so delicate, soft and intense,
It was felt like an odour within the sense.

'THE SENSITIVE PLANT' PERCY BYSSHE SHELLEY (1792–1822)

FOR many people our ancient woodlands are magical places and the sight of great perfumed carpets of bluebells bring back memories of childhood. The Bluebell means constancy in the Language of Flowers, probably referring to Endymion, Diana's lover, after whom the flower was named. It is an appropriate meaning for a flower which has the ability to reappear and spread year after year in our woods and gardens. The hanging bells in exquisite lavender blue make it one of the best-loved of all our wild flowers, more delicate than its cousin, the Hyacinth. The Bluebell has long been established in England and the Elizabethans used the starch found in the bulb to stiffen their ruffs. However the flower is best known for its fragrance, a beautiful, strong green scent, and its colour: in his sonnet on blue John Keats writes:

Blue! gentle cousin of the forest-green
Married to green in all the sweetest flowers,
Forget-me-not, the Bluebell, and that Queen
Of secrecy, the Violet . . .

BURDOCK

Arctium lappa

TOUCH-ME-NOT

Farmer, that thy wife may thrive,
Let not bur and burdock wive,

LORNA DOONE R. D. BLACKMORE (1825–1900)

BURDOCK has enormous leaves which sometimes span several yards in weedy places by the wayside and on waste land. It has several purple spiky flowerheads on one stem – the hooked balls or burs which give the plant its name. It is also sometimes known as Happy-major, Clot-bur and Hurr-burr and is the one specimen well known by small children who pull off the burs to throw at one another. The burs were the symbol for 'touch-me-not' in the Language of Flowers, for once attached to clothing or animal fur they are difficult to remove.

Shakespeare was familiar with Burdock and included it in King Lear's crown of weeds. He referred to the plant metaphorically more than once; Pandarus says in *Troilus and Cressida* of his kindred: 'ThTTThey are but burrs, I can tell you; they'll stick where they are thrown.'

It was once believed that if you ate the burs it would help things to stick in your mind.

BUTTERCUP

Ranunculus bulbosus

CHILDISHNESS, INGRATITUDE

Ye field flowers! the gardens eclipse you, 'tis true:
Yet, wildings of nature! I dote upon you,
For ye waft me to summers of old,
When the earth teemed around me with fairy delight,
And when daisies and buttercups gladdened my sight
Like treasure of silver and gold.

'FIELD FLOWERS' THOMAS CAMPBELL (1774–1844)

MANY children are introduced to Buttercups by their mothers holding the blossom underneath their chins to see if they love butter. These are the gold-cups and cuckoo-buds of Shakespeare which cover the meadows in May with dazzling golden flowers:

> When daisies pied and violets blue,
> And lady-smocks all silver-white,
> And cuckoo-buds of yellow hue
> Do paint the meadows with delight.

Ranunculus was said to be a Libyan boy dressed in green and gold who entertained the wood nymphs by singing beautiful songs. One day they tired of listening to him and turned him into a green and gold flower.

Buttercups are one of the earliest flowers to bloom in the spring, thanks to the nourishment which is stored in the bulbs. They share the spring meadows with daisies and poppies and flower right through the season. They are part of the yellow of the autumn fields, and can be seen up until deep winter alongside Herb Robert and the White Nettle.

The juice of the Buttercup inflames and blisters the skin, a trick used by beggars to gain sympathy. It has been used as a remedy to cure gout and rheumatism, and a tincture made with wine spirits is said to cure shingles and sciatica.

Clover

Trifolium pratense

INDUSTRY

Sweet bottle-shaped flower of lushy red
Born when the summer wakes her warmest breeze,
Among the meadows waving grasses spread,
Or 'neath the shade of hedge or clumping trees,
Bowing in slender stem thy heavy head.

'To a Red Clover Blossom' John Clare (1793–1864)

CHILDREN often suck the sweet flowers of Red Clover, sometimes known as Honeystalk or Sugar-plum. Its meaning, 'industry', perhaps stems from the fact that butterflies and bees feast on its nectar. The plant also has a high lime content and has been used medicinally for centuries. Old herbals maintain that it will cleanse the blood and restore fertility; a syrup made from the flowers was given to children to ease whooping cough.

The name originates from the Latin word *trifolium*, meaning 'three-leaved', and the Clover became the symbol of the Holy Trinity. The broad leaves have horse-shoe marks, which may be the origin for the lucky four-leaved Clover. Clover was once regarded as an antidote for all poisons, perhaps another reason for its 'lucky' reputation. The seventeenth-century poet Robert Herrick wrote in 'A Nuptial Song':

> Glide by the banks of virgins, then, and pass
> The showers of roses, lucky four-leav'd grass.

Cowslip

Primula veris

PENSIVENESS, WINNING GRACE

Then came the cow-slip,
Like a dancer in the fair,
She spread her little mat of green,
And on it danced she.
With a fillet bound about her brow,
A fillet round her happy brow,
A golden fillet round her brow,
And rubies in her hair.

'A CHANTED CALENDAR', SYDNEY DOBELL (1824–74)

THE Cowslip is one of the first flowers to be found in springtime on banks and in meadows and is simply named, for *primula* means first and *veris*, spring. The Cowslip is a member of the primula family and is the sister of the Primrose and the Auricula. The golden yellow flowers, drooping from tall stems, have orange flecks at the base of the petals. Shakespeare referred to these more than once as freckles, for example in this fairy song in *A Midsummer Night's Dream*:

The cowslips tall her pensioners be;
In their gold coats spots you see,
Those be rubies, fairy favours,
In those freckles live their savours . . .
I must go seek some dew-drops here,
And hang a pearl in every cowslip's ear.

In old herbals the cowslip was often referred to as Herb Peter or Key Flower because the nodding heads of the flowers were thought to symbolize St Peter's bunch of keys. The poet Hartley Coleridge (1796–1849) wrote:

The coy cowslip, though doom'd to stand
In state upon the open field,
Declines her head.

Cowslips have been made into wine since Elizabethan times, when children made them into cowslip balls and garlands for May Day. They are a welcome addition to any garden, and as a result they are not as easily found in the wild as they were once.

CRANE'S-BILL

Geranium molle

STEADFAST PIETY

Flower in the crannied wall,
I pluck you out of the crannies –
Hold you here, root and all, in my hand,
Little flower – but if I could understand
What you are, root and all, and all in all,
I should know what God and man is.

'FLOWER IN THE CRANNIED WALL', ALFRED, LORD TENNYSON (1809–92)

THERE are many different varieties of Wild Geranium, but the best known is Herb Robert, also known as Stinking Crane's-bill, due to its unattractive scent. Herb Robert was named after a Frenchman, the Abbé Robert, who founded the Cistercian Order in the eleventh century. This may also be the derivation of 'Steadfast piety' as the meaning in the Language of Flowers. Dove's Foot is another name attributed to the species, but the popular name of Crane's-bill was inspired by the beaked fruit, which resembles the bill of a crane and comes from the Greek, *geranos* (crane).

Tennyson was not the only poet to be inspired by this flower: Wordsworth discovered that the old walls and steps in front of the house at Rydal Mount in the Lake District were covered in Herb Robert:

. . . how gay
With his red stalks upon this sunny day!
And, as his tufts of leaves he spreads, content
With a hard bed and scanty nourishment
Mixed with the green, some shine not lacking power
To rival summer's brightest scarlet flower.

Dandelion

Taraxacum officinale

Oracle, Faithfulness

Dear common flower, that grow'st beside the way,
Fringing the dusty road with harmless gold,
First pledge of blithesome May,
Which children pluck, and full of pride uphold,
High-hearted buccaneers, o'erjoyed that they
An Eldorado in the grass have found,
Which not the rich earth's ample round
May match in wealth, thou art more dear to me
Than all the prouder summer-blooms may be.

Gold such as thine ne'er drew the Spanish prow
Through the primeval hush of Indian seas,
Nor wrinkled the lean brow
Of age, to rob the lover's heart of ease;
'Tis the spring's largesse, which she scatters now
To rich and poor alike, with lavish hand,
Though most hearts never understand
To take it at God's value, but pass by
The offered wealth with unrewarded eye.

'To the Dandelion' James Russell Lowell (1819–91)

If it were not so common and not so insistent on growing on ground where it is not wanted, the Dandelion would be considered a handsome flower. However, it grows plentifully throughout the year on all types of soil so farmers consider it a troublesome weed. Yet the generic name comes from the Arabic meaning salad vegetable, for the leaves are sweet when gathered in the spring and may be eaten raw in salad or boiled like spinach. They contain high amounts of vitamins and folklore maintains that if you drink a cup of

Dandelion tea each morning you will never have rheumatism.

The name Dandelion comes from the French *dent-de-lion*, for the jagged leaves resemble the teeth of a lion; this name or its equivalent may be found in nearly all the European languages. The meaning of Dandelion in The Language of Flowers is Oracle, originating from the superstition that if you blow off all the seeds on the seedhead in one breath, your wish will come true. The alternative meaning is Faithfulness and may have arisen from the plant's ability to survive and reproduce quickly.

Dog Rose

Rosa canina

PLEASURE AND PAIN

O, how much more doth beauty beauteous seem
By that sweet ornament which truth doth give!
The rose looks fair, but fairer we it deem
For that sweet odour which doth in it live.
The canker-blooms have full as deep a dye
As the perfumed tincture of the roses,
Hang on such thorns and play as wantonly
When summer's breath their masked bud discloses;
But, for their virtue only is their show,
They live unwood'd and unrespected fade;
Die to themselves – sweet roses do not so;
Of their sweet deaths are sweetest odours made.
And so of you, beauteous and lovely youth,
When that shall vade, by verse distills your truth.

'Sonnet 54' William Shakespeare (1564–1616)

The Dog Rose is one of the longest living plants known to man and growing today in a convent garden in Germany is a Dog Rose reputed to have been planted by one of Charlemagne's sons in the year 850AD. The meaning, 'pleasure and pain' surely comes from the idea that the sweet-scented Dog Rose gives so much pleasure when it is found blooming in the wild, but causes pain with its large prickles if you try to cut it.

Shakespeare was very familiar with the Dog Rose which bloomed freely in the countryside in Warwickshire. He referred to it as the Canker Rose and felt that it did not bear comparison with a

garden rose whose fragrance lingers on after it is cut and dried. He used the comparison again in *Henry IV Part 1*, when Hotspur calls it a shame:

> To put down Richard, that sweet lovely rose,
> And plant this thorn, this canker, Bolingbroke

and in *Much Ado About Nothing*, Don John says: 'I had rather be a canker in the hedge than a rose in his Grace.'

The seventeenth-century poet George Herbert said in his poem 'Providence', 'A Rose, besides his beauty, is a cure', and in Elizabethan England rosehips were made by gentlewomen into tarts and conserves, and rosehip syrup is given to children as a tonic to this day.

Foxglove

Digitalis purpurea

INSINCERITY

Deep, deep in wizardry
All the foxglove belfries stand.
Should they startle over the land,
None would know what bells they be.
Never any wind can ring them,
Nor the great black bees that swing them –
Every crimson bell, down-slanted,
Is so utterly enchanted.

Mary Webb (1882–1927)

The Foxglove has two sides to its personality. On the one hand, it is considered the flower of the fairy folk and is known in folklore as Fairy Thimbles and Fairy's Gloves, since it grows in shady dells, deep in the woods where children have always believed the fairies live. On the other hand, it has a sinister side: the freckles on the Foxglove bells were said to be the fingerprints of elves, placed there as a warning that the plant was highly poisonous. This ambivalence is reflected in two interpretations of The Language of Flowers where the Foxglove is given opposing meanings. Usually it is referred to as Insincerity, but it is also regarded as Amiability and Confiding Love.

The Foxglove is best friend to the honey-bee, for the wide bells are full of honey and the bee goes from flower to flower up the stalk, fertilizing it as it goes. Smaller insects use it as a shelter, hiding inside the bells when it rains, but no animal ever touches the Foxglove, their instinct warning them of its dangerous character.

In George Eliot's *Silas Marner*, Silas gave a simple preparation of Foxglove to the cobbler's wife who was suffering from heart disease and dropsy. The flower was widely employed by herbalists for a wide range of remedies and is still cultivated today for medicinal use.

Laura Knight

Greater Stitchwort

Stellaria holostea

Afterthought

High on the downs so bare,
Where thou dost love to climb,
Pink Thrift and Milkwort are,
Lotus and scented Thyme;

And in the shady lanes
Bold Arum's hood of green,
Herb Robert, Violet,
Starwort and Celandine;

'The Idle Flowers' Robert Bridges (1844–1930)

In April and May the lovely Greater Stitchwort with its delicate green leaves and white starry petals is one of the beauties of the hedgerow. It should not be picked, as it fades rapidly, but folklore maintained that taken with mashed acorns and wine, the Greater Stitchwort would cure

a stitch, or a pain in the side. Its botanical name comes from *stella*, the Latin word for star, in reference to the star-shaped flowers. It is sometimes referred to as Starwort, or the Satin Flower. *Holostea* was the old generic name, meaning, 'whole bones', derived from its use in ancient medicine for healing fractures.

It is stitchwort that George Eliot refers to in *The Mill on the Floss*:

The wood I walk in on this mild May day, with the young yellow-brown foliage of the oaks between me and the blue sky, the white star-flowers and the blue-eyed speedwell and the ground ivy at my feet – what grove of tropic palms, what strange ferns or splendid broad-petalled blossoms, could ever thrill such deep and delicate fibres within me as this home-scene?

For me, – she stoop'd, and, looked round,
Pluck'd a blue harebell from the ground, –
For me, whose memory scarce conveys
An image of more splendid days,
This little flower that loves the lea,
May well my simple emblem be;
It drinks heaven's dew as blithe as rose
That in the king's own garden grows;
And when I place it in my hair,
Allan, a bard is bound to swear,
He ne'er saw coronet so fair.

THE LADY OF THE LAKE SIR WALTER SCOTT (1771–1832)

Harebell

Campanula rotundifolia

— Submission, Grief —

Harebells grow plentifully in the wild, both on dry chalky grassland and in damp peaty bogs. The lilac flowers look very frail, but are surprisingly sturdy and can tolerate both heat and cold. However, they look most at home on the heather moors of Scotland and northern England and are known as the Bluebells of Scotland. *Campanula* comes from the Latin meaning 'little bell', and *rotundifolia* refers to the round leaf of the plant.

Harebells are mentioned frequently in literature. In *The Prelude*, Wordsworth told how he saw them in his travels in the north of England:

Or, not less pleased, lay on some turret's head,
Catching from tufts of grass and hare-bell flowers
Their faintest whisper to the passing breeze,
Given out,while mid-day heat oppressed the plains.

Some country folk believe that the Harebell has sinister associations and should never be pitched: for this reason it is also known as Witch Bell or Witches' Thimble. Perhaps Emily Brontë was aware of this, or perhaps it was their meaning, 'grief', which prompted her to include them in her moving ending of Wuthering Heights:

I lingered round them under that benign sky, watched the moths fluttering among the heath and harebells, listened to the soft wind breathing through the grass, and wondered how anyone could ever imagine unquiet slumbers for the sleepers in that quiet earth.

KINGCUP

Caltha palustris

DESIRE OF RICHES

Hark, hark! the lark at heaven's gate sings,
And Phoebus 'gins arise,
His steeds to water at those springs
On chalic'd flowers that lies;
And winking Mary-buds begin
To ope their golden eyes;
With everything that pretty is –
My lady sweet, arise!
Arise, arise.

CYMBELINE WILLIAM SHAKESPEARE (1564–1616)

ALTHOUGH Kingcups are known as Marsh Marigolds, they are members of the Buttercup family. *Caltha* is derived from the Greek word *kalathos*, meaning 'cup' and *palustris* is the Latin word for marsh-growing. The large golden-yellow flowers abound in the marshes and wet meadows, flowering from March to July. The plant was named in honour of the Virgin Mary, which is why Shakespeare called its blooms Mary-buds. Earlier poets associated the flower with gold, for when they bloom profusely on the river bank in the early summer they make the ground look as though it is paved with gold, hence the meaning 'desire of riches'. Tennyson in 'The May Queen' mentions the dazzling colour of Kingcups:

The wild marsh-marigold shines like fire in swamps and hollows gay.

The leaves may be cooked and eaten and the flower buds pickled and used like capers. It was believed that when Kingcups were taken into the bedroom of a young girl subject to fits, the attacks ceased.

Lady's Slipper Orchid

Cypripedium calceolus

Capricious beauty

It seemed as if the breezes brought him;
It seemed as if the sparrows taught him;
As if by secret sight he knew
Where, in far fields, the orchids grew.

'Woodnotes' Ralph Waldo Emerson (1803–1882)

THIS spectacular orchid is one of the rarest of our wild flora. It was once common enough to be sold to travellers by the roadside in the north of England, but has been so ruthlessly hunted by collectors desperate to have a specimen of their own that it is almost extinct in England as a wild flower, but still inhabits the woodlands of Europe and north Asia. The name is derived from the Greek, *kypris*, one of the names of the goddess Venus, and *podion*, meaning 'a little foot or slipper', thus becoming Venus's slipper, or Lady's Slipper. A country name is Whippoorwill Shoes.

In *Ravenshoe*, Henry Kingsley (younger brother of Charles Kingsley) wrote of the meadows near Maidenhead:

Through the lengthening grass, through the calthas, and the orchises, and the ladies' slippers, and the cowslips, and the fritillaries, through the budding flower garden which one finds in spring among the English meadows.

Lady-Smock

Cardamine pratensis

PATERNAL ERROR

At first but single,
And then in flocks,
In dell and dingle,
The Lady-Smocks
Make mist for the golden cowslip tapers,
To shine like a sunrise through morning vapours.

'A Spring Carol' Alfred Austin (1835–1913)

ALFRED Austin was made Poet Laureate in 1896. He was devoted to spring flowers. In a further poem entitled 'Is Life Worth Living?' he answers the question in the title with:

Yes, in spring,
While children in the woodlands yet
Adorn their little laps
With lady-smock and violet,
And daisy-chain their caps.

Lady-smocks prefer damp ground and flower in early April and May. Many country names of wild flowers refer to the time of year when they bloom, and though the pale blossoms of the Lady-smock last a long time, they are at their best when the cuckoo may be heard and are often known as the Cuckooflower. It is assumed that Lady-smock refers to the Virgin Mary, after whom many white flowers are named. However, shining in the sun, and so plentiful as to hide the green grass, the flowers give a silver-white effect and the name Lady-smock may recall a white cloth spread ove the fields.

Cardamine is the word used for a salad plant and Lady-smock is eaten in France, where it is said to be a stimulant and an aid to digestion. Its pale silver-white blossoms were well known to Shakespeare who included it in his pretty 'Spring Song' at the end of *Love's Labour's Lost*:

When daisies pied and violets blue,
And Lady-smocks all silver white,
And cuckoo-buds of yellow hue,
Do paint the meadows with delight . . .

Lesser Celandine

Ranunculus ficaria

Joys to come

Pansies, lilies, kingcups, daisies,
Let them live upon their praises;
Long as there's a sun that sets,
Primroses will have their glory;
Long and there are violets
They will have a place in story:
There's a flower that shall be mine,
'Tis the little Celandine.

'To the Small Celandine' William Wordsworth (1770–1850)

The Lesser Celandine thrives in shady woods and damp hedgerows and flowers early in the spring. In Elizabethan times it was also known as Pilewort. During the great Plague of London in the seventeenth century, half a handful of Celandine with powdered ivory, six spoonfuls of dragon-water and other ingredients was recommended as a remedy for the illness to the English housewife. The flowers are the colour of golden butter, hence the country names Butter-and-cheese and Golden Guineas. *Ficus* is the Latin name for fig, and refers to the fig shape of the root tubers: the roots used to be hung for luck in the cow-shed. It is likely that both the Lesser Celandine and the unrelated Greater Celandine may have been named after the Greek word for swallow, *chelidon*, because they flower when the swallows return, hence the significance of joys to come.

The flower was often praised by Wordsworth, who devoted three poems to it, and even Tennyson, writing in old age on 'The Progress of Spring', noted when

Out once more in varnish'd glory shine
Thy stars of Celandine.

Mallow

Malva silvestris

MILDNESS

The sitting down, when school was o'er
Upon the threshold of the door,
Picking from Mallows, sport to please,
The crumpled seed we called a cheese.

'THE SHEPHERD'S CALENDAR' JOHN CLARE (1793–1864)

THE common Mallow is a bushy plant with large rose-purple flowers. The flowers have clearly marked veins which are supposed to guide insects down to the honey. They bloom right through the summer and the flowers are followed by a ring of seeds, rather like a cheese. Country children in olden days ate the unripe seeds, as John Clare recalled.

Malva comes from *malakos*, the Greek word for soft or soothing, referring to an emollient obtained from the seeds. Mallows were commonly eaten by the poor in ancient Greece – Aristophanes spoke of eating mallow shoots instead of loaves of wheat. The Marsh Mallow, one of the many different species of Mallow, is the genuine origin of the sweet pink and white candy of the same name. A type of sticky toffee was made by boiling the roots of the plant. The toffee was also made into lozenges and was an old remedy for coughs.

TON ADAMS

MEADOWSWEET

Spiraea ulmaria

USELESSNESS

Where is the girl, who by the boatman's door,
Above the locks, above the boating throng,
Unmoor'd our skiff, when, through the Wytham flats,
Red loosestrife and blond meadow-sweet among,
And darting swallows, and light water-gnats,
We track'd the shy Thames shore?

'THYRSIS' MATTHEW ARNOLD (1822–88)

THIS feathery flower is also known as Queen-of-the-meadows and has a honeyed almond-like scent. The name Queen-of-the-meadows may have arisen because the plant was a favourite of Queen Elizabeth I, and its leaves, with their wintergreen scent, were used to decorate palaces and banqueting halls in summertime. The flowers and leaves were also widely used in pot-pourris, as their scent is long-lasting and mellows sweetly with age. In Anglo-Saxon times Meadowsweet was also known as Meadsweet, Meadwort and Bridewort, as it was blended with mead to produce the flavour of Greek wines, and was an important part of wedding feasts.

John Clare includes this pretty flower in his poem on summer:

The meadowsweet taunts high its showy wreath
And sweet the quaking grasses hide beneath.

MORNING GLORY

Convolvulus arvensis

WORTH SUSTAINED, OBSTINACY

Screen'd is this nook o'er the high, half-reap'd field,
And here till sun-down, shepherd, will I be.
Through the thick corn the scarlet poppies peep,
And round green roots and yellowing stalks I see
Pale blue convolvulus in tendrils creep:
And air-swept lindens yield
Their scent, and rustle down their perfum'd showers
Of bloom on the bent grass where I am laid,
And bower me from the August sun with shade;
And the eye travels down to Oxford's towers:

THE SCHOLAR GYPSY MATTHEW ARNOLD (1822–1888)

THE great trumpet flowers of Morning Glory are a common sight in a wild garden, where it winds itself around other plants – hence the country name of Bindweed. *Convolvulus* comes from the Latin, to entwine, and Morning Glory always turns in an anticlockwise direction. It is sometimes referred to as Rope-bind or Withy-wind and is hated by gardeners for its habit of strangling other plants. It is very difficult to eliminate, hence its meaning. The flowers are almost unscented, but are a favourite of all types of insect, being abundant in honey. In his 'Summer Images', John Clare made a reference to this:

The gay convolvulus, wreathing round the thorn,
Agape for honey showers.

Oxeye Daisy

Chrysanthemum leucanthemum

PATIENCE

A tuft of daisies on a flowery lay
They saw, and thitherward they bent their way;
To this both knights and dames their homage made,
And due obeisance to the daisy paid.
And then the band of flutes began to play,
To which a lady sang a virelay:
And still at every close she would repeat
The burden of the song, 'The daisy is so sweet',
'The daisy is so sweet', when she begun,
The troop of knights and dames continue'd on.

'THE FLOWER AND THE LEAF' JOHN DRYDEN (1631–1700)

WHILST the Oxeye Daisy is part of the *Chrysanthemum* family, it is also called the Moon Daisy or Marguerite. Possibly because it resembles a full moon it is often associated with stormy weather and bunches of its flowers used to be hung over barn doors to ward off lightning. Its name comes from the Greek, *chrysos*, 'gold', and *anthemom*, 'a flower', for the Oxeye Daisy has a yellow disc in the centre of the flower. It flowers in meadows and fields in midsummer, and has long grown in England, being mentioned by the fourteenth-century poet Chaucer as one of his favourite flowers.

Robert Bridges wrote in 'The Idle Flowers':

And where high grasses wave
Shall great Moon-daisies blink.
With Rattle and Sorrel sharp
And Robin's ragged pink.

Pasqueflower

Pulsatilla pratensis

YOU HAVE NO CLAIM

The spring is crowned and stoled
In purple and gold . . .
Deep in the Chiltern Woodland grows
The purple pasque anemone.

'St George's Day' John Davidson (1857–1909)

THE plant acquired its name because the bright green dye which comes from both the flowers and leaves was often used to decorate Easter eggs (from the French word *Pasque*). It was also known as Dane's Blood due to an old English superstition that they grow only where Danish blood has been split.

Pasqueflower is used widely by homeopaths, especially in the treatment of measles. It also affects the heart rate, and its name reflects this – *Pulsatilla* means 'pulsator': it has to be used carefully as it is, in fact, poisonous. The name Laughing Parsley was given to it in the belief that anyone eating it would die of laughter. *Pratensis* means field-growing, and sometimes it is hard to find these silky, violet flowers, as their short stems are often hidden by surrounding grass.

PERIWINKLE

Vinca minor

EARLY FRIENDSHIP

Through primrose tufts in that green bower,
The periwinkle trailed its wreaths;
And 'tis my faith that every flower
Enjoys the air it breathes.

'LINES WRITTEN IN EARLY SPRING' WILLIAM WORDSWORTH (1770–1850)

THE meaning of this plant must have derived from the long spreading stems which the Periwinkle extends as it happily spreads across the ground. It is one of our oldest flowers and in the Middle Ages was a symbol of death and immortality. Criminals wore a garland of periwinkles at their execution and it was known in Italy as Death's Flower. It was also said to be a herb of Venus, the goddess of love, and as a result was taken to increase fertility. It is a valuable medicinal plant and was used as a remedy for various ailments including high blood pressure, and as a gargle to cure a sore throat.

Vinca originates from the Latin, *vincio*, 'to bind', alluding to the long tough runners which were frequently used to make wreaths, or to tie around the calf of the leg to prevent cramp. Culpeper the herbalist maintained that 'the leaves of periwinkle eaten by man and wife together, will cause love between them'.

Nineteenth-century writer Mary Russell Mitford paid tribute to the periwinkle in the autumn chapter of *Our Village*, her series of essays on rural life:

Ah! here is the hedge along which the periwinkle breathes and twines so profusely, with its evergreen leaves shining like the myrtle, and its starry blue flowers. It is seldom found wild in this part of England; but when we do meet with it, it is so abundant and so welcome, – the very robin-redbreast of flowers, a winter friend.

POPPY

Papaver rhoeas

FANTASY, SLEEP, SILENCE

We are slumberous poppies,
Lords of Lethe downs,
Some awake, and some asleep
Sleeping in our crowns.
What perchance our dreams may know,
Let our serious beauty show.

Central depth of purple,
Leaves more bright than rose,
Who shall tell what brightest thought
Out of darkness grows.
Who, through what funereal pain
Seeks to love and peace attain?

'SONGS OF THE FLOWERS' JAMES HENRY LEIGH HUNT (1784–1859)

NO-ONE can fail to be impressed by the show of Poppies in our cornfields in summertime, and most of our great poets and novelists have made reference to this infamous flower. The meaning of the scarlet field Poppy is fantasy or fantastic extravagance, whereas the significance of the oriental or white opium Poppy is silence and sleep. It is to this that most of the poets refer. In the second stanza of his 'Ode to Autumn', Keats writes:

> What hath not seen thee oft amid thy store?
> Or on a half-reap'd furrow sound asleep,
> Drowsed with the fume of poppies?

All Poppies are narcotic and opium was imported from the East long before the plant became established in our gardens and meadows. Shakespeare was obviously familiar with the opium poppy as revealed in *Othello*:

Not poppy, nor mandragora,
Nor all the drowsy syrups of the world,
Shall ever medicine thee to that sweet sleep
Which thou ow'dst yesterday.

The country nickname for the Poppy is Headache as a warning to those who smell the heavy odour of opium when the Poppy is in bloom.

Primrose

Primula vulgaris

EARLY YOUTH, SADNESS

Welcome, pale primrose! starting up between
Dead matted leaves of ash, and oak, that strew
The every lawn, the wood and spinney through,
'Mid creeping moss, and ivy's darker green:
How much thy presence beautifies the ground;
How sweet thy modest unaffected pride
Glows on the sunny banks, and wood's warm side,
And where thy fairy flowers in groups are found.

'Rural Poems' John Clare (1793–1864)

The inimitable colour of the wild Primrose has been described by writers and artists as yellow, green and even white, but in verse they are always referred to as pale. Perhaps this has influenced their meaning in The Language of Flowers which is Early Youth or Sadness. In *A Winter's Tale*, Shakespeare referred to them as 'pale primroses that die unmarried'.

Primroses used to grow abundantly in the wild and bunches of flowers were sold on the streets of London in Victorian times. As medical knowledge increased, so demand grew for the roots of the primrose plant; enterprising thieves dug them up and sold them, with the result that there are no wild Primroses left on London's Primrose Hill today.

Edward Waite

Queen Anne's Lace

Daucus carota

Festivity

O, Brignal banks are wild and fair,
And Greta woods are green,
And you may gather garlands there
Would grace a summer queen.

'Rokeby' Sir Walter Scott (1771–1832)

Queen Anne's Lace grows freely and makes a great show in the meadows in May. It is the wild form of the cultivated carrot and is one of many umbelliferous plants with elegant parasol-like flower heads. It is sometimes referred to as Cow Parsley. Its lacy clusters of white flowers are very decorative and it was frequently used to decorate homes and churches for weddings and parties, hence the meaning of the name. The common name, Queen Anne's Lace, comes from the pretty white blossoms, reminiscent of the lacy head-dresses which Queen Anne liked to wear.

The Greeks valued it as an aphrodisiac, and called it *Philtron*. Herbalists believed that epilepsy could be cured by eating the one dark red or purple floret at the centre of the white flower-head. Folklore tells us that Queen Anne was making lace when she pricked her finger; the purple floret represents her blood.

Ragged-Robin

Lychnis flos-cuculi

WIT

Let never maiden think, however fair
She is not fairer in new clothes than old.
And should some great court-lady say, the Prince
Hath pick'd a ragged-robin from the hedge,
And like a madman brought her to the court,
Then were ye shamed, and, worse, might shame the Prince
To whom we are beholden.

'The Marriage of Geraint' Alfred, Lord Tennyson (1809–92)

A mass of Ragged-robin in full flower is a wonderful sight in the wild. It is one of the May flowers of the marsh, scattered over the damp meadow. Clumps of white froth are commonly found on the plant, produced by the larvae of leaf hoppers. This is known as cuckoo-spit and is the reason why another country name for the plant is Cuckoo Flower. *Lychnis* is Greek for lamp, a reference to the red, serrated flowers which grow abundantly on tall stems over two feet high.

In 'The Picture', Samuel Taylor Coleridge has a vision of a lady who plucks:

The heads of tall flowers that behind her grow,
Lychnis, and willow-herb, and foxglove bells.

SNAKE'S-HEAD FRITILLARY

Fritillaria meleagris

PERSECUTION

I know what white, what purple fritillaries
The grassy harvest of the river fields
Above by Eynsham, down by Sandford, yields
And what sedged brooks are Thames's tributaries

'THYRSIS' MATTHEW ARNOLD (1822–88)

THE Fritillary is a type of wild Tulip with drooping, single flowers. It was introduced into England in the seventeenth century by Huguenots fleeing from French tyranny, and as a result the meaning of this beautiful flower is persecution. It quickly became naturalized in the damp meadows of the Thames valley, which is where Matthew Arnold found them. Its delicate single bells have given rise to many country names, particularly Snake's-head because of the resemblance it bears to the scales of a snake. *Fritillaria* is the Latin for dice-box, as the markings on the flower resemble a chess-board, often used for games of dice. *Meleagris* is the Greek name for guinea-fowl, and the flower-head looks like the grey spotted feathers of the bird, or Ginny-hen, another common name for this pretty nodding flower. It was fashionable in France as early as the fifteenth century, where it was known as *Narcissus caparonius*, named after Noel Capron, an apothecary from Orleans who was murdered in the massacre of St Bartholomew's Day in 1572. Small wonder that the meaning of this fragile flower became persecution.

Snowdrop

Galanthus nivalis

Hope

. . . Brother, joy to you!
I've brought some snowdrops; only just a few,
Cheerful and hopeful in the frosty dew
And for the pale sun's sake.

'The Months' Christina Rossetti (1830–94)

It is thought that Snowdrops were brought to Britain by monks in the fifteenth century, as they may be frequently found in old monastery gardens. They were planted there to provide blooms for Candlemas Day, the Feast of the Purification of the Virgin on the first day of February, which perhaps explains the names by which they are known in folklore, Candlemas Bells and February Fair-maids.

The Latin name comes from the Greek *galanthus* meaning 'milkflower' and, *nivalis*, 'snowy', for this brave little flower often has to push its way up through the snow, blooming whilst it is still winter. It is one of the most eagerly awaited wild flowers, as its arrival heralds the coming of spring, and it has been a source of inspiration for some of our greatest poets, including Wordsworth:

To a Snowdrop

Lone Flower, hemmed in with snows, and white as they
But hardier far, once more I see thee bend
Thy forehead as if fearful to offend,
Like an unbidden guest. Though day by day
Storms, sallying from the mountain-tops, waylay
The rising sun, and on the plains descend;
Yet art thou welcome, welcome as a friend

Whose zeal outruns his promise! Blue-eyed May
Shall soon behold this border thickly set
With bright jonquils, their odours lavishing
On the soft west-wind and his frolic peers;
Nor will I then they modest grace forget,
Chaste Snowdrop, venturous harbinger of Spring,
And pensive monitor of fleeting years!

SOLOMON'S SEAL

Polygonatum multiflorum

— CONCEALMENT, DISCRETION —

Consider the lilies of the field, how they grow; they toil not, neither do they spin: And yet I say unto you, That even Solomon in all his glory was not arrayed like one of these.

THE GOSPEL ACCORDING TO ST MATTHEW

KING Solomon, the king of Israel who reigned in the tenth century, was renowned for his wisdom and is said to have given his seal of approval to this plant. A more credible theory is that of Dioscorides, who maintained that when the roots of the plant were dried and laid on wounds, they healed very quickly. Thus the ancient name of Solomon's Heal became Solomon's Seal. The name *Polygonatum* comes from *polys*, meaning 'many' and *gonu* meaning 'a small joint'. This refers to the many joints in the rootstock which are said to resemble the impression of a seal upon wax. Country folk also refer to the plant as Ladder-to-heaven because the leaves grow alternately up the slender curving stem like a miniature ladder. A herbalist writing in the sixteenth century suggested that if the roots were applied whilst fresh they would remove by dawn any bruise acquired by a wilful wife.

The meaning in the Language of Flowers is one of secrecy between the sender and the recipient. With its dark green foliage, arched stems and hanging white bells it is a most romantic plant, and would be welcome in any bouquet. It grows in dry shady woodlands and is a sister of Lily of the Valley.

Sweet Violet

Viola odorata

Modesty

I know a bank whereon the wild thyme blows,
Where oxlips and the nodding violet grows.

A Midsummer Night's Dream William Shakespeare (1564–1616)

It is curious that so familiar and well-loved a flower as the Violet has no English name of its own. *Viola* is a Latin word describing the colour of the flowers and *odorata* means 'sweet smelling', for of all the different species of the plant, the Sweet Violet, with its dry, powdery scent, is the favourite. The white species is particularly fragrant but also difficult to find: the meaning comes from the humble stance of the plant which demurely hangs its head and hides away in the shade.

The Sweet Violet was so esteemed by the ancient Greeks that the flower became the symbol of Athens. It was cultivated by them to sweeten food, and by the fifteenth century was to be found in every monastery garden, to be used in both food preparation and medicine. It was used to relieve melancholy and as a cure for headaches and insomnia, even for babies, the flowers being laid on the pillow when they went to bed at night.

The Sweet Violet has been mentioned by many poets through the ages, but it was Shakespeare who wrote of it as a flower of consequence, referring to it as 'forward', as it is one of the earliest flowers to bloom in the spring:

The forward violet thus did I chide –
Sweet thief, whence didst thou steal thy sweet that smells,
If not from my love's breath?

Tansy

Tanacetum vulgaris

I DECLARE WAR AGAINST YOU

At stool-ball, Lucia, let us play
For sugar-cakes and wine:
Or for a tansy let us pay,
The loss, or thine, or mine.

HESPERIDES ROBERT HERRICK (1591–1674)

THE tall, flat, yellow flower-heads of Common Tansy may be found in the English countryside throughout the summer, the name being derived from the Greek, *athanatos*, meaning 'immortal'. The meaning in the Language of Flowers, 'I declare war against you', probably refers to the bitterness of the plant. At Eastertime the leaves were shredded, beaten up with eggs and made into small, flat Tansy-cakes. These Tansies were eaten on Easter Sunday and represented the bitter herbs of the Passover. Samuel Pepys noted in his diary in the year 1666 that he ate a tansy, and they were also among the delicacies served at the coronation feast of James II.

Teasel

Dipsacus sylvestris

MISANTHROPY

And where men never sow,
Have I my Thistles set,
Ragwort and stiff Wormwood
And straggling Mignonette,

Bugloss and Burdock rank
And prickly Teasel high,
With Umbels yellow and white,
That come to kexes dry.

'THE IDLE FLOWERS' ROBERT BRIDGES (1844–1930)

THE Teasel has an egg-shaped head of lilac-coloured blossom covered in prickles. It grows up to six feet high, and pools of water collect at the base of the long stem where the leaves join. One traveller noted in his wildlife journal that the leaf-basin nearest the ground will hold as much as two or three cups of water, hence the genus name which comes from the Greek, *dipsao*, 'to thirst'. Cottagers would say that the water had special properties and if applied regularly could make you as beautiful as Venus, hence the name Venus' Basin. Others believed that it would remove warts.

The name Teasel comes from its use in the clothing industry. The Teasel has a seed-head with hooks on the spines that are used for teasing – raising a nap on woollen cloth. In *The Fleece*, the eighteenth-century poet John Dyer writes of the noisy mill:

Soon the clothier's shears,
And burler's thistle, skim the surface sheen.

As a tribute to the power of nature, it is interesting to observe that no machine has ever been invented which can compete with the Teasel and that one firm could use as many as 20,000 Teasel-heads in one year.

Thistle

Onopordum acanthium

Retaliation

Rank weeds, that every art and care defy,
Reign o'er the land, and rob the blighted rye;
There thistles stretch their prickly arms afar,
And to the ragged infant threaten war,

The Village George Crabbe (1754–1832)

This magnificent architectural plant grows up to nine feet tall and can look as handsome in the garden as in the wild. The whole plant is hoary with a white cottony down, which has resulted in the thistle being called the Cotton or Woolly Thistle. Its meaning in the Language of Flowers obviously comes from the fact that the leaves are cruelly spined, but those who are willing to brave this may eat the stalks and the heart of the head. An old remedy implies that a distillation of Cotton Thistle applied to a bald head will restore a full head of hair.

Since the reign of James III the thistle has been the national emblem of Scotland. Legend says that when the Danes invaded Scotland and were about to mount a surprise attack at night, a Dane stepped on a thistle with his naked foot. The Scots were awakened by his cries and were able to defend themselves. The thistle was the inspiration for the national motto, *Nemo me impune lacessit* ('no-one irritates me unscathed'), and those who wear the thistle will be protected.

TOADFLAX

Linaria vulgaris

PRESUMPTION

'Butter and eggs!' I can hear her cry
All over the country-side
'Butter and eggs, who'll buy, who'll buy?'
It follows me far and wide.

ANONYMOUS

THE bright yellow flowers tinged with orange look like tiny snapdragons, but their country name is Butter and Eggs. *Linaria* is derived from the Latin word *linum*, meaning 'flax', which the leaves resemble before the plant flowers. It is sometimes referred to as Flaxweed by cottagers. The name Toadflax comes from the similarity between the mouth of the flower and the wide mouth of a toad. The plant was used as a remedy for bubonic plague, and was called Bubo, the word for a plague swelling, and this may have been mistaken for the Latin *bufo* meaning 'toad'. The meaning in the Language of Flowers probably originates from the fact that this small yellow-flowered plant can easily become a pest in the garden, as tiny pieces of root quickly grow into new plants.

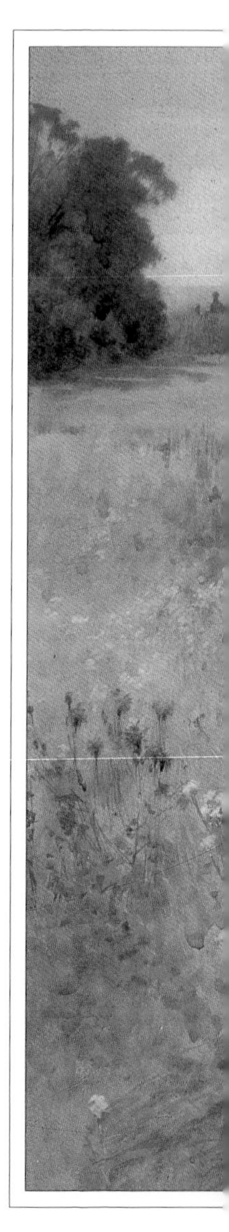

WILLOW-HERB

Epilobium hirsutum

PRETENTION

. . . for see, ah! see,
The sportive tyrant with her left hand plucks
The heads of tall flowers that behind her grow,
Lychnis and willow-herb, and foxglove bells:
And suddenly, as one that toys with time,
Scatters them on the pool! Then all the charm
Is broken – all that phantom-world so fair
Vanishes, and a thousand circlets spread,
And each mis-shape the other. Stay awhile
Poor youth, who scarcely darest lift up thine eyes!

'THE PICTURE' SAMUEL TAYLOR COLERIDGE (1772–1834)

THE tall Willow-herb may be found in ditches, woody banks and wet places; masses of tall purple-red flowers can be seen towards the end of summer, the scented leaves growing on downy stems covered with short hairs.

The flowers appear to grow on the seed-pod, which gave rise to the name, derived from the Greek, *epi*, 'upon', and *lobos*, 'a pod'. When bruised the leaves and top-shoots have a delicate scent which resembles scalded codlings (unripe apples), hence its country name of Codlings and Cream. The seeds of the Willow-herb have long seed hairs which used to be made into wicks for candles. It is said to be St Anthony's herb of antiquity.

The Willow-herb is featured in Tennyson's poem 'The Brook':

> With many a curve my banks I fret
> By many a field and fallow,
> And many a fairy foreland set
> With willow-weed and mallow.

Wood Anemone

Anemone nemorosa

Sickness

Then came the wind-flower,
In the valley left behind, pale,
As a wounded maiden,
With purple streaks of woe,
When the battle has rolled by,
Wanders to and fro,
So totter'd she,
Dishevelled in the wind.

'A Chanted Calendar' Sydney Dobell (1824–74)

The Wood Anemone is a frail-looking flower, but hardy and not afraid of cold spring days. They are also called Windflowers for they will survive on a windswept hillside and are some of the earliest to appear in the spring. As Wordsworth wrote:

But her humility is well content
With one wild floweret (call it not forlorn)
Flower of the winds, beneath her bosom worn
Yet more for love than ornament.

They form a carpet in the woods and at night and in wet weather they close their sepals and droop their pretty heads to protect their pollen. Folklore describes how the fairies curl up inside for protection, having first pulled the curtains around themselves. Wood Anemones have a delicate sweet scent but a bitter juice, poisonous to animals. They were sometimes used for the treatment of paralysis, which may account for their meaning.

Cath.B.Gulley.

WOODBINE

Lonicera periclymenum

BONDS OF LOVE

Sleep thou, and I will wind thee in my arms . . .
So doth the woodbine the sweet honeysuckle
Gently entwist; the female ivy so
Enrings the barky fingers of the elm.
O, how I love thee! How I dote on thee!

A MIDSUMMER NIGHT'S DREAM WILLIAM SHAKESPEARE (1564–1616)

THIS is the true flower of the country lane and is quite the loveliest of our wild climbers. The name *Lonicera* was given to it by the Swedish naturalist and physician Linnaeus in honour of Adam Lonicer, a physician and naturalist of the sixteenth century. Country people called it Woodbine or Woodbind from its habit of twining its tough stems, later used to bind brooms. The flowers open when warmed by the sun, and give off a strong honey-sweet fragrance, hence the name Honeysuckle. It is one of the oldest plants in the hedgerow and a great favourite of poets and novelists. With its heady scent, twining stems and rich creamy yellow flowers it often paints a romantic picture for the reader. It was mentioned by Chaucer in *The Knight's Tale*, and Robert Herrick wrote to his lover Phyllis in *Hesperides*:

The soft, sweet moss shall be thy bed
With crawling woodbine overspread;
By which the silver-shedding streams
Shall gently melt thee into dreams.

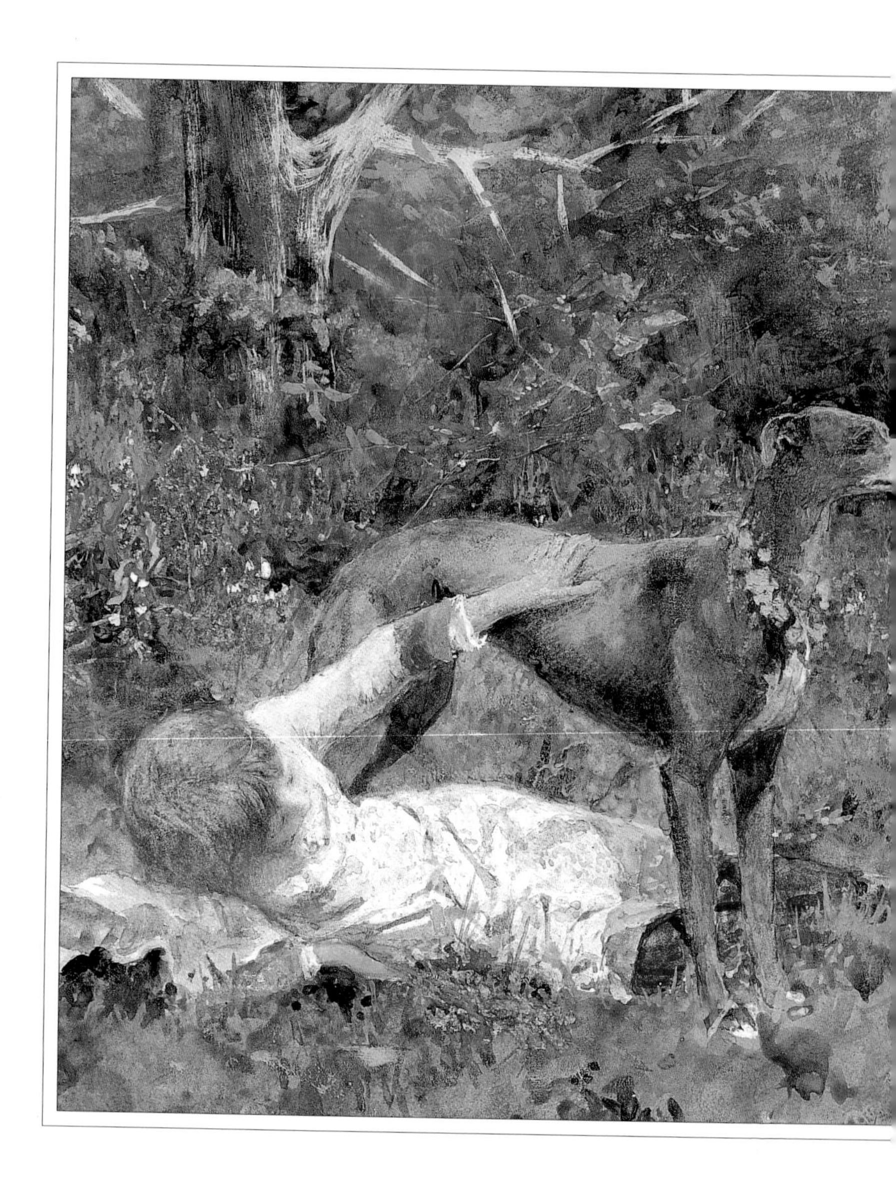

Wood Sorrel

Oxalis acetosella

—Joy, Maternal tenderness—

Thick on the woodland floor
Gay company shall be,
Primrose and Hyacinth
And frail Anemone,
Perennial Strawberry-bloom,
Woodsorrel's pencilled veil,
Dishevel'd Willow-weed
And Orchis purple and pale.

'The Idle Flowers' Robert Bridges (1844–1930)

Wood Sorrel is also known by country folk as Hallelujah, and with trefoil-like leaves it has always been suspected that this is the leaf of the Irish shamrock. This fragile-looking plant with charming, delicate white blossoms tinged with pink or purple is often found in the deep shade of beechwoods. The plant itself is quite protective, closing itself up into a small mound at night or if it rains or is touched, rather like a mother folding her arms around her child, hence the meaning. It also droops its blossoms and folds its leaves in stormy weather. The genus name comes from the Greek *oxys*, meaning 'sour' and the old generic name *acetosella*, meaning 'vinegar salts'. The leaves may be eaten as a salad or made into syrups and sauces which, true to their name, have a rather tart taste. These are used as a blood tonic or to treat scabies. Another old herbal remedy recommends pressing the red juice from the leaves and making a syrup to cure mouth ulcers.

YARROW

Achillea millefolia

WAR

And by the dusty road
Bedstraw and Mullein tall,
With red Valerian
And Toadflax on the wall,

Yarrow and Chicory,
That hath for hue no like,
Silene and Mallow mild
And Agrimony's spike.

'THE IDLE FLOWERS' ROBERT BRIDGES (1844–1930)

THE Yarrow, or Milfoil, is one of the commonest wild plants, and continues flowering well into the autumn when few other blossoms are out. It takes its botanical name from Achilles, the Greek warrior, who is said to have cured the wounds of his soldiers with the leaves of the plant during the Trojan wars. *Millefolia*, or thousand-leaved, refers to the many hair-like segments of its foliage. The name Yarrow is derived from the Greek *hiera*, or holy herb, for it contains medicinal properties. Indeed, the country names Staunchweed and Carpenter's Weed arose because fresh leaves were used to staunch bleeding caused by sharp carpenters' tools. Nosebleed is another name attributed to it. The Elizabethan poet Drayton, describing a herbalist at work, writes of 'The Yarrow, wherewithal he stops the wound-made gore'.

Yarrow was considered one of the herbs of the Devil, known as Devil's Plaything, and was one of the ingredients of magic spells. It was also used as a preventative against baldness, and a tisane made from the leaves is reputed to eliminate melancholy and calm fevers.

PENHALIGON'S BLUEBELL

The Language of Wild Flowers is scented with Penhaligon's Bluebell, a scent which has always been the symbolic note of spring. Created in 1978, it is a beguiling fresh, green scent reminiscent of English woods where carpets of flowers grow under the trees in springtime. The scent of Bluebell is true to the flower yet quite unique and has become recognized around the world as a classic English perfume.

Sheila Pickles

Acknowledgements

Bridgeman Art Library, London:
p4 Lily of the Valley and Cowslips: Ursula Hodgson/Private Collection; p5 Girl in a Landscape with Bluebells: John Clayton Adams/Whitford & Hughes, London; p13 Helleborus, Viridis: Claude Aubriet/Naural History Museum, London; p14-15 In the Grass: Arthur Hughes/Sheffield City Art Galleries; p17 The Vision of Endymion: Sir Edward John Poynter/Manchester City Art Gallery; p18-19 The Burdock Bush: Otto Marseus Van Schrieck/Radichtchev Museum, Saratov, USSR; p20 Wild Flowers: William Charles Thomas Dobson/Oldham Art Gallery, Lancs.; p22 Red Clover. Border from: *The Hours of the Virgin*, School of Jean Bourdichon/ British Library, London; p25 A Lady Sewing at a Window: Francis John Wyburd/ Christopher Wood Gallery, London; p27 Crane's Bill: Marie Anne/Victoria & Albert Museum, London; p35 Making a Posy: William Bromley/Christie's, London; p37 Canterbury Bell: George-Dyonis Ehret/Earl of Derby Collection, Suffolk; p40 Slipper Orchid from *The Botanical Cabinet*, Loddiges/Lindley Library, Royal Horticultural Society, London; p44-45 Friends and Foes: Joseph Kirkpatrick/Christopher Wood Gallery, London; p50 The Flower Seller: Emily Mary Osborn/Gavin Graham Gallery, London; p58 Wild Flowers, The Artist's Wife Hebe at West Wittering, Sussex, 1905: Harold Waite/Private Collection; p63 In Primrose Time (Abinger Hammer): Edward Wilkins Waite/Private Collection; p70-71 Among the Greenery: Olga Wisinger-Florian/Christie's; p73 Lesbia and her Sparrow; Sir Edward John Poynter/Christie's, London; p74-75 Ballaugh, Isle of Man: Henry John Yeend King/Oscar & Peter Johnson Ltd., London; p78-79 Thistledown: Mary Louise Breakell/Gavin Graham Gallery, London; p81 Three Little Girls: William Affleck/Christopher Wood Gallery, London; p83 Picking Flowers: Henry John Yeend King/Bonhams, London; p85 Memories; Catherine B Gulley/City Museum and Art Gallery, Bristol; p92-93 The Bluebell Glade: Ernest Walbourn/Beaton-Brown Fine Paintings, London.

Burford Gallery, Burford, Oxon:
p88 The Champion's Garland: Lionel Percy Smythe.

David Museum Gallery, London:
p33 Foxgloves: Dame Laura Knight © Reproduced by permission of Curtis Brown Group. London.

Fine Art Photographs, London:
p2 Among the Bluebells: Beatrice Parsons; p10 Feeding the Calves: Ernest Walbourn; p12 Gathering Wild Flowers: Alfred Glendening; p16 Woodland Bluebells: Daniel Sherrin; p23 Best Friends: Harold Harvey; p29 Summer Love: Edward Niczky; p31 Children Picking Wild Roses: William Kay Blacklock; p36 Summer in Arcadia: Albert Durer Lucas; p38-39 The Parasol: Arthur Hacker; p41 Queen for a Day; Paul Falconer Poole; p43 Spring in the Orchard: Alfred William Parsons; p47 A Summer's Day, Newlyn, Cornwall: Thomas Mortimer; p48-49 Spring Blossom: John Clayton Adams; p53 Portrait of a Little Girl: Charles Goldsborough Anderson; p56 Reading Aloud on a River Bank: Edward Ridley; p60-61 Harvest Time on the Estate: Adolf Muller; p65 A Posy of Pretty Flowers: Carl Bauerle; p87 Picking Honeysuckle: Sophie Anderson; p90-91 In the Orchard: Valentine Davie.

Glasgow Museum & Art Gallery, Kelvingrove, Glasgow:
p69 The Coming of Spring: Edward Hornel; p77 Pauvre Fauvette: Jules Bastien-Lepage.

Natural History Museum, London:
p54 Pulsatilla pratensis – Pasque Flower.

Private Collection, London:
p12 Agrimony; p21 Buttercup; p29 Dandelion; p30 Dog Rose; p32 Foxgloves; p34 Greater Stitchwort; p42 Lady's Smock; p57 Periwinkle; p66 Ragged Robin; p67 Snake's Head Fritillary; p74 Tansy; p80 Toadflax; p82 Willow Herb; p89 Wood Sorrel.

Private Collection, USA/Richard Green Gallery, London:
p7 A Morning Walk: Arthur Hacker.

Cover: Wild Flowers, The Artist's Wife Hebe at West Wittering, Sussex, 1905 (detail); Harold Waite, Private Collection/Bridgeman Art Library, London.

First published in Great Britain in 1995 by
PAVILION BOOKS LIMITED
26 Upper Ground
London SE1 9PD

Designed by Bernard Higton
Picture research by Lynda Marshall

A CIP catalogue record for this book is available from the British Library

ISBN 1-85793-066-5

Printed in Hong Kong by Imago

2 4 6 8 10 9 7 5 3 1

This book may be ordered by post direct from the publisher.
Please contact the Marketing Department.
But try your bookshop first.